TEC

Y0-BVQ-593

Butterfly Gardens

Jennifer B. Gillis

Rourke

Publishing LLC

Vero Beach, Florida 32964

www.rourkepublishing.com

PHOTO CREDITS: All photos © Lynn M. Stone

Editor: Robert Stengard-Olliges

Cover design by Michelle Moore.

imprint
TK

Dedication: The publisher wishes to thank Ulrich Hartmond, Director Butterfly House and Insectarium; Leon Bradford, Lead Entomologist; Leiana Guerrero, Director of Family and School Experiences; and Richard Stickney, Butterfly Curator; of the Museum of Life and Science, Durham, NC, for their expertise in the preparation of this publication.

Library of Congress Cataloging-in-Publication Data

Gillis, Jennifer Blizin, 1950-
  Butterfly gardens / Jennifer Blizin Gillis.
      p. cm. -- (Field trips)
  Includes index.
  ISBN 978-1-60044-560-6
  1. Butterfly gardens--Juvenile literature. I. Title.
  QL544.6.G55 2008
  595.78'9--dc22
                                    2007017259

Printed in the USA

CG/CG

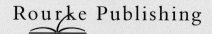

Rourke Publishing

www.rourkepublishing.com – rourke@rourkepublishing.com
Post Office Box 3328. Vero Beach. FL 32964

Table of Contents

Wings under Glass

It's fun to watch butterflies in motion as they flutter from flower to flower in a summer meadow. Where can you watch butterflies in other seasons? You can see them in a butterfly house, also called a **conservatory**. A conservatory is a giant glass room filled with plants and trees. People visit conservatories to learn about plants and insects.

Being in a well-planned butterfly house is ▶ almost like being outdoors.

Who Will You Meet?

It takes a lot of people to run a butterfly house. **Educators** meet school groups and teach them about the butterflies. A **curator** is the person who is in charge of the conservatory, and who makes sure everything is working as it should. An **entomologist** studies insects and butterflies, and makes sure the butterflies have the food and conditions they need to live in the conservatory.

An educator talks to students about ▶ how butterflies use plants.

7

Special Exhibits

Before you go into the conservatory, you may see some special **exhibits**. There may be pictures to help you learn the names of some of the butterflies you will see. You may learn about plants and weather in countries the butterflies come from. Some butterfly houses also have exhibits of insects. You may be able to pet a giant roach or millipede!

Students gather at an exhibit of ▶ butterfly *chrysalises*.

9

In the Rain Forest

When you walk into the conservatory, you are walking into a **rain forest**. At about 80 degrees F (26.6 degrees C) and 80 percent **humidity**, the steamy air causes peoples' glasses to fog up. Tall trees, flowers, and plants from **tropical** countries surround you. There may be hummingbirds or other birds flying about, along with hundreds of beautiful butterflies. If you stand very still, some may land on you.

▲
The stars of the butterfly house are
the beautiful insects themselves.

11

Make-Believe World

Gardeners and **botanists** create the rain forest one tree or plant at a time. They fill the floor of the conservatory with tons of soil just like the soil in a rain forest. Then they plant trees, shrubs, and vines from tropical countries. They water the conservatory from the floor to the ceiling everyday, just as showers water real rain forests each day. Every few minutes, special machines near the floor fill the air with **mist**.

Mist from machines keeps the ▶ rain forest plants damp.

13

Special Delivery!

Butterflies for the conservatory are raised on butterfly farms in Asia, South America, or Africa. Each butterfly is inside a **chrysalis**. Farmers remove the chrysalises from bushes, put them in boxes, and send the boxes to the conservatory. When the boxes arrive, curators gently unpack the chrysalises and glue them to strings. Each day a few butterflies emerge, or come out.

Butterflies will emerge from these chrysalises. ▶

Waking Up

New butterflies have damp, droopy wings, and at first they cannot fly. The curator collects them in a special basket. Now it's time for a butterfly **release**. The curator takes off the lid of the basket as a crowd gathers. The butterflies act sleepy and crawl slowly around. Then they begin to flutter away from the basket, landing on anything nearby—even people.

An educator releases newly emerged butterflies.

Feeding

New butterflies begin feeding right away. Some of them feed on tropical fruits, such as pineapples and oranges. Some of them feed on brightly colored flowers. The butterflies do not actually eat. Instead, they poke their long tongues—called a proboscis—into the fruit or flowers and suck up a juice called nectar.

A butterfly probes for nectar with its ▶ straw-like proboscis.

Life in the Conservatory

Butterflies live for just about two weeks and spend their days feeding or flying. Birds that live in the conservatory eat any butterfly eggs they find. If these eggs hatched, hungry caterpillars could quickly eat all the plants. Curators must also make sure that butterflies don't get outside, where they might harm plants and crops.

This butterfly just emerged from its ▶ chrysalis. It will live only a few days.

21

Did You Know?

- Each butterfly in a conservatory costs about $2.00. Some butterfly houses spend more than $50,000 each year to buy new butterflies.

- Caterpillars are truly "very hungry." Some can eat 86 times as much as they weighed when they were just eggs.

- Butterflies look for nectar from sunrise to sunset. When night falls, they rest. As soon as the sun comes up, they begin feeding again.

Glossary

botanist (BOTT ehn ist) — scientist who studies plants

chrysalis (KRIS uh liss) — tough covering in which a butterfly changes from a pupa to a fully grown butterfly

conservatory (kuhn SER vuh to ry) — large room or house made of glass in which plants can grow year round

curator (KYURE ay ter) — person whose job it is to take care of something in a museum

educator (EJ you kate r) — person at a museum, planetarium, or other public place who teaches people about the exhibits

entomologist (en toh MOLL oh jist) — scientist who studies insects

exhibit (eg ZIB it) — something put in a place where many people can see it

humidity (hyu MID it ee) — the amount of moisture in the air

mist (MISST) — tiny droplets of water in the air

rain forest (RAN for ist) — forest in an area where the weather is warm and damp and where there is a lot of rain during the year

release (ree LEES) — to let go

tropical (TROP uh kul) — places close to an imaginary line around the earth called the equator, where the weather is always hot

Index

Further Reading

Kelly, Irene. *It's a Butterfly's Life*. Holiday House, 2007.

Stidworthy, John. *Queen Alexandra's Birdwing. The World's Largest Butterfly*. Bearport Publishing, 2007.

Thatcher, Rebecca. *Threat to the Monarch Butterfly*. Mitchell Lane Publishing, 2007.

Websites to Visit

www.butterflywebsite.com

www.amnh.org/exhibitions/butterflies/garden.html

www.arnoldsbutterflyhaven.com/

www.flmnh.ufl.edu/butterflies/

www.foremostbutterflies.com

About the Author

Jennifer B. Gillis is an author and editor of nonfiction books and poetry for children. A graduate of Gilford College in North Carolina, she has taught foreign language and social studies in North Carolina, Virginia, and Illinois.